Shapes

Heinemann

First published in Great Britain by Heinemann Library
an imprint of Heinemann Publishers (Oxford) Ltd
Halley Court, Jordan Hill, Oxford OX2 8EJ

MADRID ATHENS PARIS
FLORENCE PRAGUE WARSAW
PORTSMOUTH NH CHICAGO SAO PAULO
SINGAPORE TOKYO MELBOURNE AUCKLAND
IBADAN GABORONE JOHANNESBURG

Designed by The Point
Cover design by Pinpoint Design
Printed in China
Produced by Mandarin Offset
99 98 97 96 95
10 9 8 7 6 5 4 3 2 1

ISBN 0431 06893 3

British Library Cataloguing in Publication Data
Kirkby, David
Shapes. - (Maths Live Series)
I. Title II. Series
516.15

Acknowledgements
The author and publisher wish to acknowledge, with thanks,
the following photographic sources:

Hutchison p14; David Muscroft p42 centre; Allsport/S. Bruty p12; Ace Photo Agency p12;
Photo Resources p22; Courtesy Zanussi Ltd p23 top; Zefa pp32, 38, 39; Marcus Alexander p42 bottom;
Roger Scruton pp18, 19, 24; Courtesy of Fired Earth p14 bottom; Trevor Clifford p23 centre, 25

The publishers would also like to thank the following for the kind loan of equipment:
NES Arnold Ltd; Polydron International Ltd.

Note to reader: words in **bold** in the text are explained in the glossary on page 44.

CONTENTS

Two-dimensional (2D) shapes are flat and can be drawn on paper. We often call them **plane shapes**.

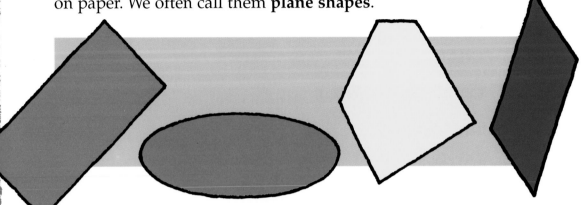

Here are some drawings of two-dimensional shapes. *Do you know any of their names?*

You can measure how long they are and how wide they are. You cannot measure how thick they are. Two-dimensional shapes have **length** and **width**. The length and width are their two **dimensions**.

The straight lines which are used to draw a shape are called its **sides**. Most two-dimensional shapes have straight sides, but some have curved sides, like the oval shape above.

The corner of a shape is called a **vertex**. If we are talking about more than one vertex, we describe them as **vertices**.

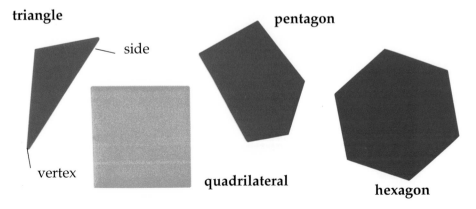

The triangle has 3 sides and 3 vertices. *How many sides and vertices do the other shapes have?*

Three-dimensional (3D) shapes have **thickness** as well as length and width. We often call them **solid shapes**.

FACTBOX			
	Length	**Width**	**Thickness**
2D shapes	✓	✓	✗
3D shapes	✓	✓	✓

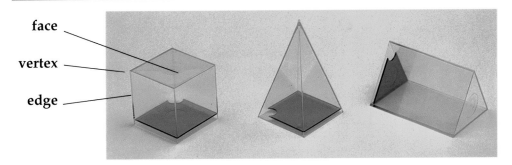

The corners of three-dimensional shapes are also called vertices. The flat part of the shapes are called **faces**, and the straight lines around them, which join the vertices, are called **edges**. The pyramid has 5 vertices, 5 faces and 8 edges.

Can you say how many vertices, faces and edges the other shapes above have?

So the two-dimensional shapes have vertices and sides, and the three-dimensional shapes have vertices, faces and edges.

FACTBOX				
	Side	**Vertex**	**Edge**	**Face**
2D shapes	✓	✓	✗	✗
3D shapes	✗	✓	✓	✓

TO DO:

A Swiss mathematician, Leonard Euler, found a rule for three-dimensional shapes. He said that, if you count the number of vertices, faces and edges, then these totals fit the rule:

vertices + faces = edges + 2.

Check to see if this is true.

2 POLYGONS

A **polygon** is a two-dimensional shape with straight sides. Polygons have special names based on their number of sides.

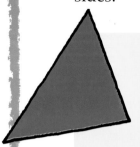
triangle

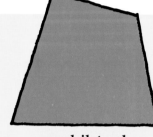
quadrilateral

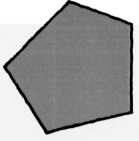
pentagon

hexagon

FACTBOX		
Name	**Sides**	**Vertices**
Triangle	3	3
Quadrilateral	4	4
Pentagon	5	5
Hexagon	6	6
Heptagon	7	7
Octagon	8	8
Nonagon	9	9
Decagon	10	10

Can you name each of these shapes?

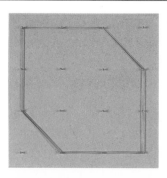

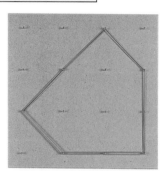

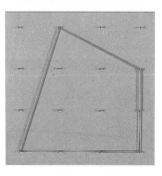

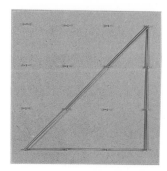

When two sides of a polygon meet, they make an **angle**. A triangle has 3 sides and 3 angles. A pentagon has 5 sides and 5 angles.

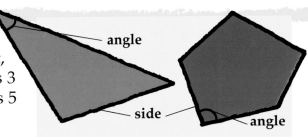

The sides sometimes meet at a wide angle, and sometimes meet at a narrow angle. Polygons can have some sides of equal length, and can have some angles of equal size.

If all the sides of a polygon are the same length, and all its angles are the same size it is called a **regular polygon**. If not, it is called an **irregular polygon**.

What do you call a regular four-sided polygon?

TO DO:

Make some polygon knots

To make a pentagonal knot:
• start with a long strip of paper
• fold it loosely as shown
• pull at the two ends.

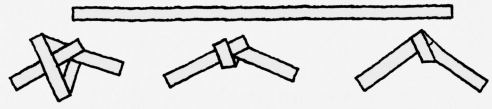

To make a hexagonal knot:
• start with two long strips of paper
• fold them as shown below
• intertwine them and pull the two ends of both strips.

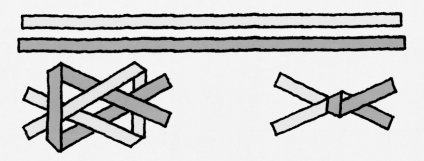

7

3 TRIANGLES

A **triangle** is a two-dimensional polygon with 3 sides.
If an object is shaped like a triangle, we describe its shape
as **triangular**.

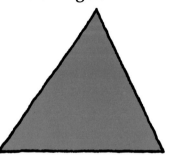

We see triangular shapes all around us.

Many road signs are
triangular. There is even
a musical instrument
called a triangle.

Some roofs have triangular shapes.
Can you see any in this picture?

CHALLENGE:

There are 8 triangles in this drawing. Can you find them?

Can you draw a shape which has 12 triangles?

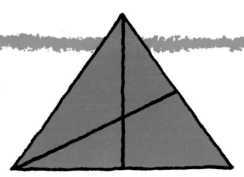

TO DO:

The triangle game

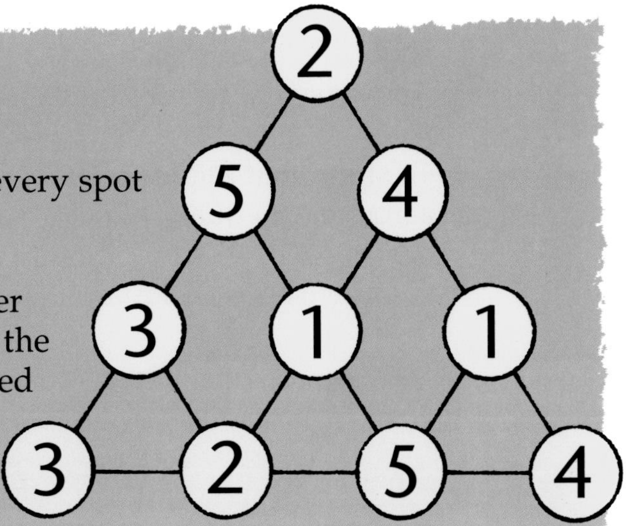

You need 9 counters.
Start by placing a counter on every spot except one.

To move, you jump one counter over another, along the line to the empty spot beyond. The jumped counter is removed.

Continue until you are unable to move. Then add up all the numbers you can see, not covered by a counter. This is your score.

Play several games.
What is your best score?

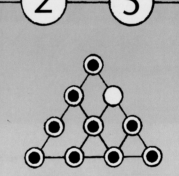

CHALLENGE:

You need a set of 12 straws.
Here is how to make 2 triangles using 5 straws.

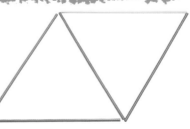

Can you:
• make 2 triangles with 6 straws?
• make 3 triangles with 7 straws?
• make 3 triangles and make 4 triangles with 9 straws?
• make 4 triangles with 10 straws?
• make 5 triangles with 11 straws?
• make 4 triangles and make 5 triangles with 12 straws?

 TYPES OF TRIANGLE

A triangle which has all 3 sides the same
length is called an **equilateral triangle.**
If the 3 sides are the same length,
it follows that all 3 angles must also
be the same size.

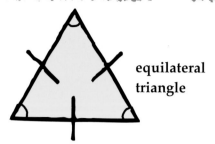

equilateral
triangle

To show that the sides are the same length, we draw one
short line across each of the equal sides, or sometimes we
draw two short lines on each side.

To show that angles are all the same size, we draw one arc
across each equal angle, or sometimes we draw two arcs
across each. To show that an angle is a right-angle, we
complete a small square inside the angle.

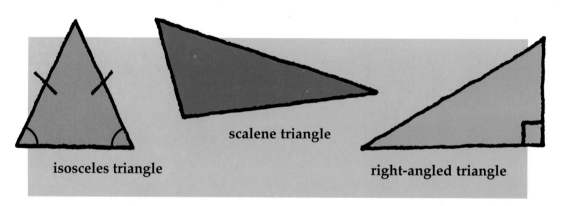

scalene triangle

isosceles triangle

right-angled triangle

Isosceles triangles have 2 sides the same length.
They have 2 equal angles. These are the angles at the feet
of the equal sides. The sides of **scalene triangles** are all of
different lengths. A triangle which has a right angle is
called a **right-angled triangle**. This factbox summarizes
the properties.

FACTBOX		Number of sides equal	Number of angles equal	Right angle
Equilateral		3	3	0
Isosceles		2	2	1 possible
Scalene		0	0	1 possible
Right-angled		0 or 2 possible	2 possible	1

TO DO:

Make an equilateral triangle from a paper circle

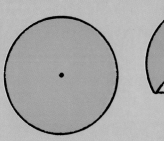 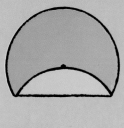 

Start with a paper circle. Mark its centre.
• Fold from any point to the centre.
• Fold to the centre again, from one end of the fold.
• Then fold the last part, and you have made an
  equilateral triangle.

CHALLENGE:

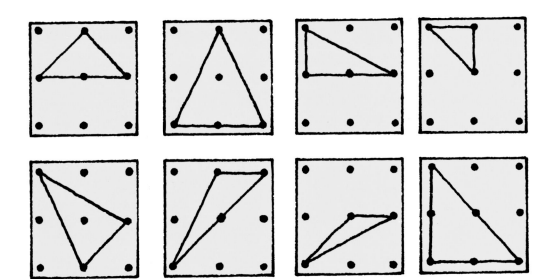

These are the 8 different triangles which can be made on a
3 x 3 pinboard.

How many of the triangles can you name?
How many triangles can you make on a 4 x 4 pinboard?

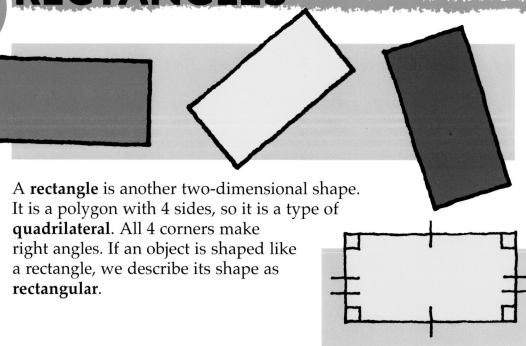

A **rectangle** is another two-dimensional shape. It is a polygon with 4 sides, so it is a type of **quadrilateral**. All 4 corners make right angles. If an object is shaped like a rectangle, we describe its shape as **rectangular**.

CHALLENGE:

Many sports pitches have marked rectangles. How many rectangles can you see on this tennis court?

There are many rectangular shapes to be seen, both inside and outside our houses. How many can you see in this picture?

The longer pair of sides measure the length of the rectangle. The shorter pair of sides measure the width of the rectangle. This rectangle has a width 3 cm and length 5 cm. We say its size is 3 by 5.

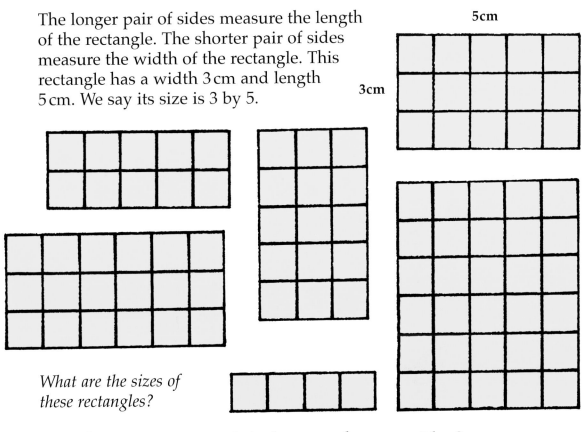

What are the sizes of these rectangles?

Note that a 3 by 5 rectangle is the same shape as a 5 by 3 rectangle.

TO DO:

Make some 2 by 1 rectangles, cut from card.

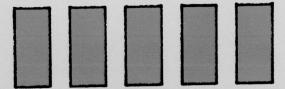

Investigate how many different ways you can place four of them inside a 2 by 4 rectangle. Here are two ways:

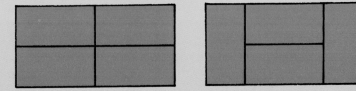

Can you find any more?
Find different ways of placing five inside a 2 by 5 rectangle.

6 SQUARES

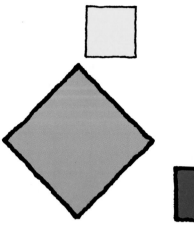

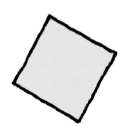

A **square** is a special rectangle. So it is another type of quadrilateral. It has 4 sides, but they are all the same length. As it is a special rectangle, the 4 corners of a square are also right-angled.

Many towns have a square space in their centre, known as the town square. Markets are often held in these squares, one day a week.

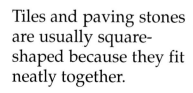

Tiles and paving stones are usually square-shaped because they fit neatly together.

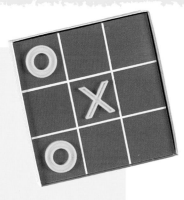

Many games are played on square-shaped boards.
How many small squares are there on the chessboard?

CHALLENGE:

There are 14 squares in this 3 by 3 square.
Can you find them?

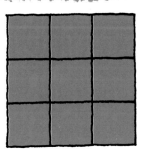

TO DO:

How can you make a square when you cannot
measure the sides?

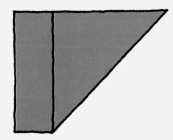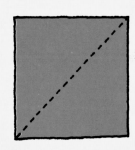

- Start with a rectangular piece of paper.
- Fold one corner so that it meets the other side.
- Draw a straight line along the edge.
- Open out the paper, and cut along the straight line.
- You now have a square piece of paper.

7 PARALLELOGRAM & RHOMBUS

A **parallelogram** is a two-dimensional shape with 4 sides. So it is another type of quadrilateral.

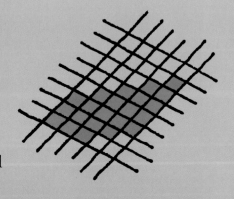

The opposite sides are the same length and parallel to each other. The pairs of opposite angles are also equal. To show that lines are parallel, we draw one arrow, pointing in the same direction on each parallel line. If we need to show another set of parallel lines, we draw two arrows on each line.

A parallelogram can be made by 'squashing' a rectangle. Here are some different parallelograms.

 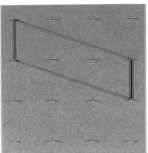 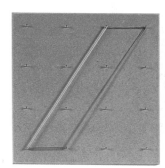 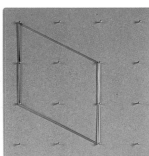

TO DO:

Draw a pattern of parallelograms

- Draw two straight lines on each edge of a ruler.
- Slide the ruler down to draw another parallel line, and so on.
- Turn the ruler so that it crosses the set of parallel lines, and use the same method to draw another set of parallel lines.

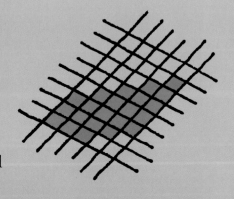

Make a pattern by colouring parallelograms.

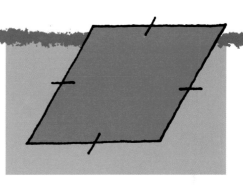

A **rhombus** is a special parallelogram. Its 4 sides are all the same length. Both the rhombus and the parallelogram are examples of quadrilaterals because they are polygons with 4 sides.

A rhombus can be made by squashing a square, just as a parallelogram can be made by squashing a rectangle. In fact, a rectangle is a right-angled parallelogram and a square is a right-angled rhombus.

 CHALLENGE:

- Start with a card rectangle.
- Mark a point on the top edge, then draw two lines as shown.
- Cut out the three pieces.

Can you arrange the pieces to make a parallelogram?
Then can you make a different parallelogram?
What other shapes can you make?

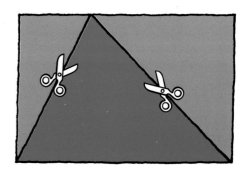

8 TRAPEZIUM

A **trapezium** is a two-dimensional shape with 4 sides. It is another type of quadrilateral.

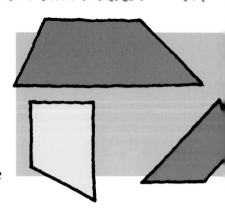

Whereas the parallelogram and rhombus have two pairs of parallel sides, the trapezium has one pair of opposite parallel sides. If we are talking about more than one trapezium, then we call them trapezia.

Many roof tops have sides which are trapezium-shaped.
How many trapezia can you see in the photograph?

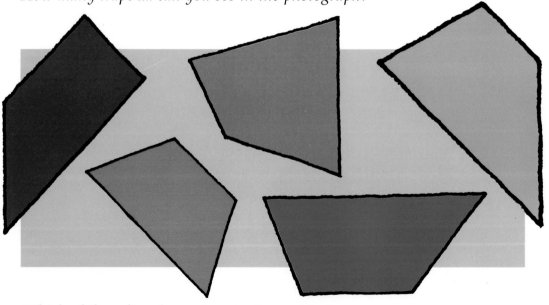

Which of these five shapes is not a trapezium?
Which are the parallel sides of the four trapezia?

If you look carefully, there are lots of trapezium shapes in this gate. There are some which are shaped like this – this is called a **right-angled trapezium** because two of the angles are right-angled.

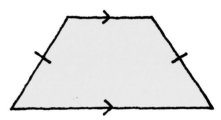

This trapezium is called an **isosceles trapezium** because its non-parallel sides are the same length.

CHALLENGE:

- Start with two equal-sized squares of card.
- Mark the mid-point of the side of one of the squares. Join it to an opposite corner.
- Cut along the line, so that you now have three pieces, labelled A, B and C.

By joining the pieces together, can you make a trapezium using
– A and B
– B and C
– A and C
– A, B and C?

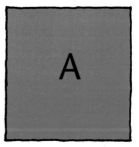
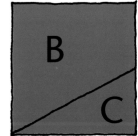

19

⑨ QUADRILATERAL

Any polygon which has 4 sides is called a **quadrilateral.**

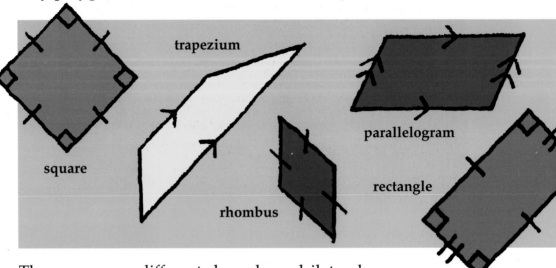

There are many different shaped quadrilaterals:
- a **rectangle**, whose opposite sides are the same length and whose angles are all right-angled
- a **square**, which is the special rectangle whose 4 sides are all the same length
- a **parallelogram**, which has two pairs of opposite parallel sides
- a **rhombus**, which is the special parallelogram whose 4 sides are all the same length
- a **trapezium**, which has one pair of parallel sides.

A **kite** is another type of quadrilateral.
It has two pairs of equal sides.

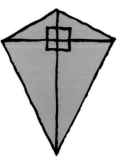

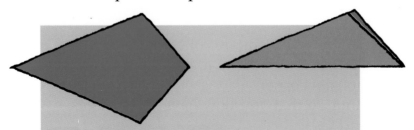

It can be folded in half to make two identical triangles.

When you draw the diagonals of a kite they always meet at right-angles, and divide the kite into four right-angled triangles.

Which of these are not quadrilaterals?
What are the names of the quadrilaterals?

 CHALLENGE:

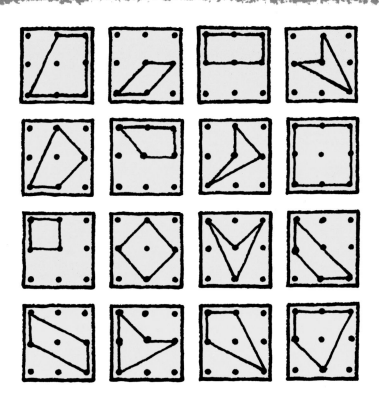

There are 16 different quadrilaterals which can be made on a 3 x 3 pinboard. How many of the quadrilaterals can you name?

10 CIRCLES

A **circle** is a plane shape.
It is a curved line with every point on
the line exactly the same distance from
a fixed point. The fixed point is called
the **centre** of the circle. If an object is
shaped like a circle, we say it is
circular.

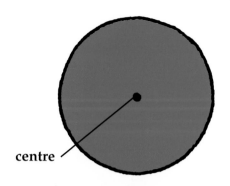

centre

The circle has been an interesting shape for many
thousands of years. It is the shape that influenced the
invention of the wheel.

TO DO:

Road signs are of different
shapes. Some are circular. All
circular road signs have a
common meaning. Find out
what this is.

There are many circular shapes in this picture. *How many can you see?*

An instrument for drawing circles is called a **pair of compasses.**

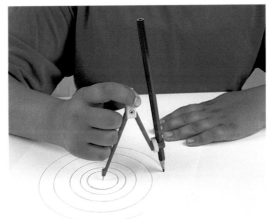

By moving the arms of the compasses but keeping the point fixed, you can use them to draw a whole set of circles which have the same centre. These are called **concentric circles.**

If a circle is sliced exactly in half, then each half is called a **semi-circle.** Some archways are **semi-circular.**

TO DO:

Draw a circle with cotton and a pencil

- Tie a piece of cotton around a pencil.
- Tie the other end to a drawing pin.
- Place a piece of paper on a drawing board, fix the drawing pin and draw your circle.

11 PARTS OF CIRCLES

The distance around the curved part of a circle is called its **circumference.**

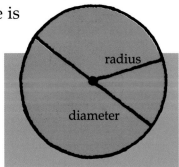

The length of the line which cuts the circle exactly in half, passing through the centre is called its **diameter.** The distance from the centre of the circle to any point on the boundary is called the **radius** of the circle. The radius is half the diameter.

radius

diameter

The circumference of a circle is about three times its diameter. So if you can measure the diameter of a wheel, multiply this by 3 to find the circumference of the wheel. This will tell you how far the bicycle will travel in one complete turn of the wheel.

TO DO:

Measure the circumference of a coin by rolling

- Draw a straight line.
- Start by marking a point on the edge of the coin.
- Gently roll the coin along the straight line, noting the starting position of the mark on the coin.
- When this mark comes back to its starting position, stop rolling the coin.
- Mark the distance the coin has rolled along the line. This will be the circumference of the coin.

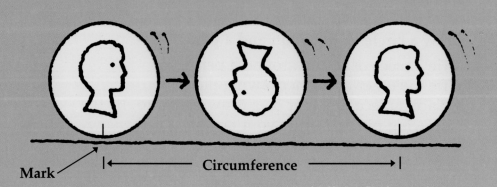

Mark ◄— Circumference —►

Another way of measuring the circumference of a circle is to use some cotton. For example, to find the circumference of the circular end of a lid from a jar, you wrap a piece of cotton round the lid. Then, stretching the cotton straight, you measure its length with a ruler. This will be the circumference of the lid.

CHALLENGE:

Find a circular lid. Measure its diameter. Guess the circumference. Then use cotton to measure the circumference to see how good your guess was.

Any straight line which joins two points on the circumference of a circle is called a **chord**. Chord comes from a Latin word meaning 'string'. A chord divides the circle into two **segments**. Any part of the circumference of the circle is called an **arc**. Arc comes from a Latin word meaning 'bow'.

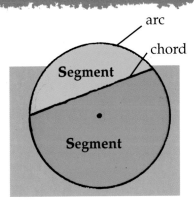

TO DO:

This circle has 4 points marked on it, which makes 4 arcs. When the points are joined, it is possible to draw 6 chords. Find out how many arcs and chords there are when the circle has 5 points.

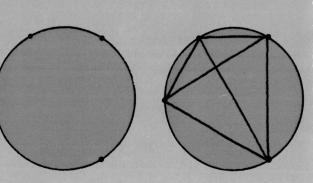

POLYHEDRON

A **polyhedron** is a solid three-dimensional shape with faces which are polygons. If we are talking about more than one polyhedron, we describe them as **polyhedra.**

Here are a set of different polyhedra. Study the shapes of the faces. *Can you name some of them?* Polyhedra have special names based on their number of faces.

The best known polyhedra are listed in the factbox.

FACTBOX	
Name	**Faces**
Tetrahedron	4
Pentahedron	5
Hexahedron	6
Octahedron	8
Decahedron	10
Dodecahedron	12
Icosahedron	20

You will remember that two-dimensional shapes with straight sides are called polygons. We also saw that if a polygon has all of its sides the same length, and its angles the same size, it is called a regular polygon.

If all the faces of a polyhedron are the same regular polygon, it is called a **regular polyhedron.** If not it is called an **irregular polyhedron.**

There are only five regular polyhedra. They are:

- the regular **tetrahedron**, with 4 equilateral triangle faces
- the regular **hexahedron**, with 6 square faces (this is a cube)
- the regular **octahedron**, with 8 equilateral triangle faces
- the regular **dodecahedron**, with 12 pentagon faces
- the regular **icosahedron**, with 20 equilateral triangle faces.

CHALLENGE:

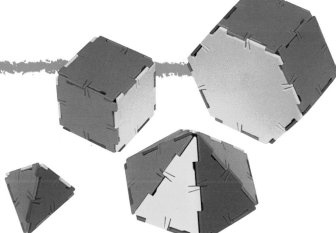

How many regular polyhedra are in this photograph? Can you name them?

Some polyhedra are beautiful to look at, and can be made from card. One way is to draw an outline of the joined faces on a piece of card. The outline is called a **net**. To make the polyhedron, you cut out the net then score along the lines, so that they will fold. Finally, glue the tabs to make your solid.

TO DO:

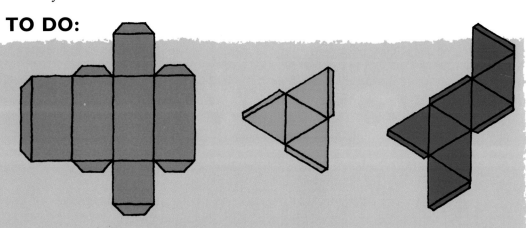

Can you imagine the shapes which can be made from these nets? Draw one of the nets on card, then make the polyhedron.

CUBES

A **cube** is a three-dimensional shape.
It has 6 identical square faces.
It has 8 vertices and 12 edges.
If an object is shaped like a cube, we
describe its shape as **cubic**.

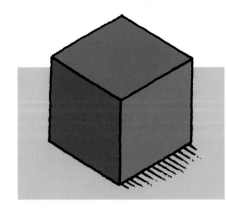

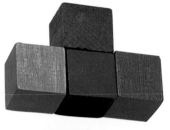

Toy building bricks are
cubic because they fit
neatly together,
without leaving any
gaps. Here are three
different buildings
made from four cubes.
*Is it possible to make any
more from four cubes?*

TO DO:

Plait a cube using squared paper

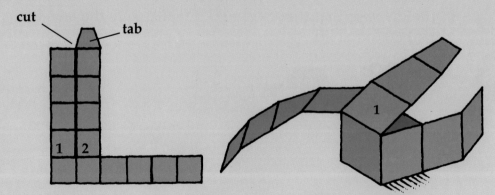

cut   tab

1   2

1

- Start by drawing and cutting out this outline on paper.
  Make the squares 5cm long.
- Cut it out along the thick line, and crease the edges of
  the squares so that they fold the same way.
- Plait the 1-square over the 2-square.
- Continue plaiting, and finally tuck in the tab to make
  your cube.

The small cubes all have edges which are 1 centimetre long. They are called **cubic centimetres**. The open cube has edges which are 10 centimetres long. *How many cubic centimetres do you think can fit inside the open cube?*

CHALLENGE:

Solve the inside-out puzzle.

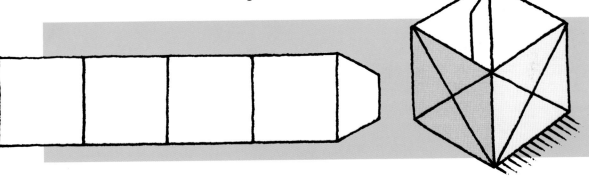

- Start by cutting out a strip of four squares from thin white card, with a tab at the end of one of the squares.
- Colour one side of the strip.
- Now draw and fold along both diagonals of each square.
- Glue the tab to make a hollow cube, so that the coloured faces are on the outside of the cube, and the white faces are on the inside.

To solve the puzzle, you need to turn the cube inside out, so that the coloured faces are on the inside, and the white faces are on the outside. Don't force it – it can be done!

14 NETS OF CUBES

A **net** is a drawing which can be cut and folded to make a three-dimensional shape. Here is a net of a cube. It can be drawn with squares, cut out, then folded along the lines to make a cube shape.

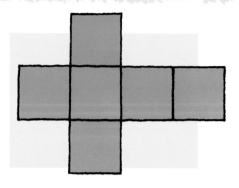

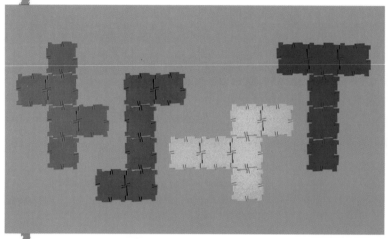

There are many different nets which will fold to make a cube. Here are four.

 TO DO:

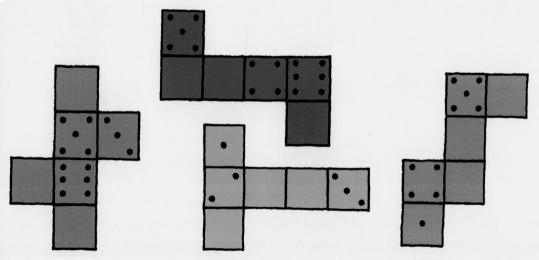

These are nets to make cubic dice. The opposite faces of a cubic dice always have a total of 7 spots. Draw the nets, work out the number of spots on the blank faces, then put them in on your drawing.

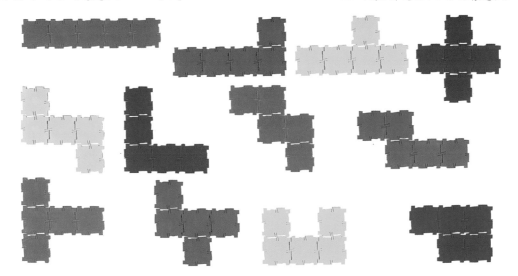

Some of these twelve nets will build an open cube.
An open cube is a cube shape with one face missing.

How many of the nets will fold to make an open cube?

You can test them by making them with squared paper,
then folding them.

 TO DO:

Make a cubic calendar

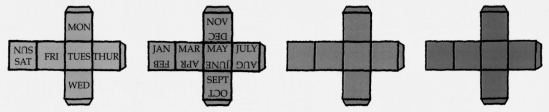

You need four cubes.
- On the faces of one cube, write the days of the week.
- On another cube, write two months on each face.
- Make two 'number' cubes to show the date.
- Put the four cubes together and the calendar will show
  the day, date and month.

Find out how you need to number the two 'number'
cubes, so that it is possible to show every date in a month.

15 CUBOIDS

A **cuboid** is another three-dimensional shape. It has 6 rectangular faces.

A cube is a special cuboid, in which all these faces are squares.

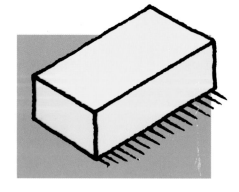

These packets are cuboids. The top and bottom of a cuboid have the same rectangle shape. The front and back also have the same shape. So do the two ends.

A solid with 6 faces is called a hexahedron. A cuboid is an example of a hexahedron. A cube is a regular hexahedron.

Many people live in a block of flats. The block is often cuboid shaped, and so are the flats.

The cuboid is the most common three-dimensional shape. When you go to the shops for food, you see lots of cuboids.

These cuboids have been built with cubes. *How many cubes are needed to make each cuboid?*

This factbox gives a summary of the properties of a cuboid.

| FACTBOX | | | | |
Name	Faces	Edges	Vertices	Shape of Faces
Cuboid	8	12	8	Pairs of identical rectangles (could include squares)
Cube	8	12	8	Squares

CHALLENGE:

With 24 bricks it is possible to build some different shaped cuboids. Here are two. Can you find four more?

1 by 2 by 12

2 by 2 by 6

How many cuboids can you build with 36 bricks?

16 PYRAMIDS

A **pyramid** is a shape with a pointed top, and a flat base. Most pyramids have a flat base which is square shaped. These are called **square-based pyramids.** If the base is triangular, then the pyramid is called a **triangular-based pyramid**. Similarly there are **pentagonal-based pyramids**, **hexagonal-based pyramids**, and so on.

The ancient stone pyramids in Egypt are examples of square-based pyramids.

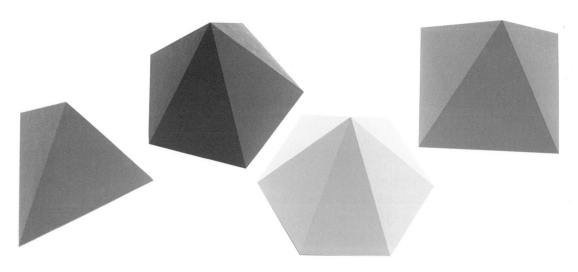

Here are some pyramids.
*Which is **triangular-based**, which is **square-based**, which is **pentagonal-based**, and which is **hexagonal-based**?*

The sloping faces of all pyramids are triangular. *How many faces does each pyramid have?*

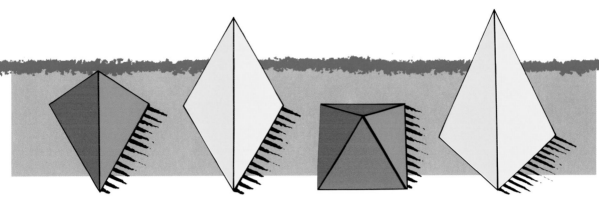

Look at the triangular faces of the pyramids. One of the square-based pyramids has faces which are equilateral triangles, the other has faces which are isosceles triangles. The same is true for the two triangular-based pyramids. As the size of the triangular faces becomes longer, the pyramid becomes more pointed.

TO DO:

Make a square-based pyramid from a net

To draw the net:
Start by drawing an 8cm square. Set a pair of compasses to 8cm. Draw short arcs, with the compass point on each vertex of the square.

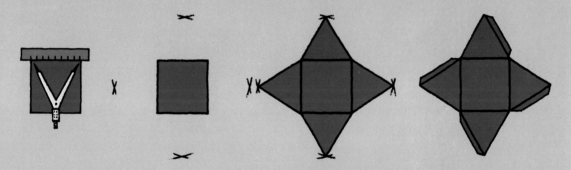

Draw lines from the vertices to the point where the arcs meet. Draw tabs along the four edges as shown. Cut out the net, score along the lines, fold and glue the tabs.

CHALLENGE:

Make two of these square-based pyramids. Put them together to make a regular octahedron. Draw spots on the 8 faces to make a dice.

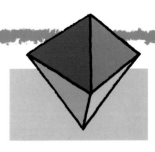

PRISMS

A **prism** is a three-dimensional solid which has the same shape at each end.

If the shape at each end is a triangle, the prism is called a **triangular prism.** If the shape at the end is a pentagon, the prism is called a **pentagonal prism.** If the shape at the end is a hexagon, the prism is called a **hexagonal prism.** All the sides, or faces of a prism are rectangles.

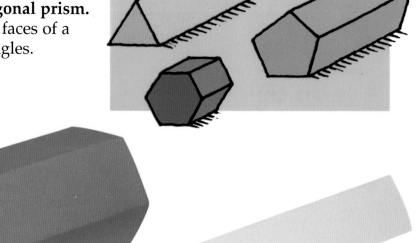

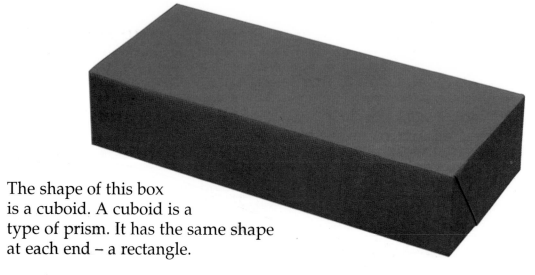

This is an example of a hexagonal prism and a triangular prism.

The shape of this box is a cuboid. A cuboid is a type of prism. It has the same shape at each end – a rectangle.

Are these boxes prisms? What sort of prisms are they?

CHALLENGE:

Five of these six nets will make a prism, which ones?

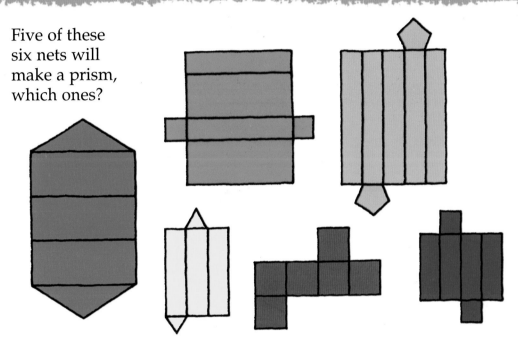

TO DO:

Make a triangular prism kaleidoscope

- You need three rectangular mirrors, or shiny pieces of card.
- Join the mirrors, reflective side inwards, with sticky tape to make a triangular prism.
- Cover one end of the prism with tracing paper
- Place some small pieces of coloured paper through the other end of the prism. What pattern can you see?

Try making some different patterns.

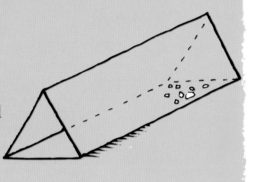

18 CONE AND CYLINDER

A **cylinder** is a prism with circular ends. If an object is shaped like a cylinder, we say it is **cylindrical**.

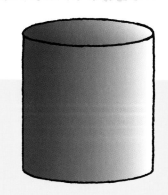

Most pipes are cylindrical.

Which of these tins are cylindrical?

Cylinders are all around us.

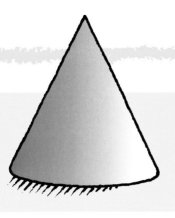

A **cone** is circular at one end, and pointed at the other. It is a pyramid with a circular base. If an object is shaped like a cone, we say it is **conical**.

This lampshade is conical, but without the point. It is part of a cone.

TO DO:

Make a cone from a sheet of paper

- Start with a circular piece of paper.
- Draw a straight line from the centre of the circle to the edge, and cut along the line.
- Curl the paper into a cone, and seal it with a piece of sticky tape.

Can you make a cylinder from a rectangular sheet of paper?

CHALLENGE:

There are 4 three-dimensional shapes whose names begin with the letter 'c'.
Can you name them?

TETRAHEDRON

A triangular-based pyramid is called a **tetrahedron.**
If we are talking about more than one tetrahedron, we describe them as **tetrahedra**.

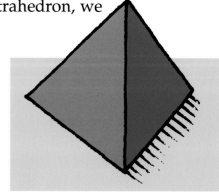

This regular tetrahedron has 4 faces which are identical equilateral triangles, meaning that all the triangles are the same size. This means that all the edges of the tetrahedron are the same length.

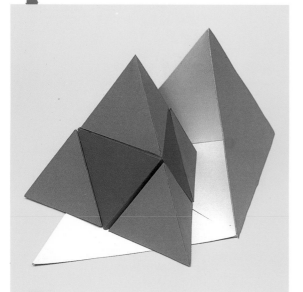

If you place four identical regular tetrahedra together with an octahedron with the same sized edge, they can be arranged to make a larger tetrahedron.

TO DO:

Make a tetrahedron

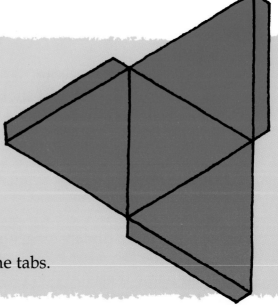

- You need an equilateral triangle template.
- Draw this net and tabs.
- Cut it out, score along the lines, fold and glue the tabs.

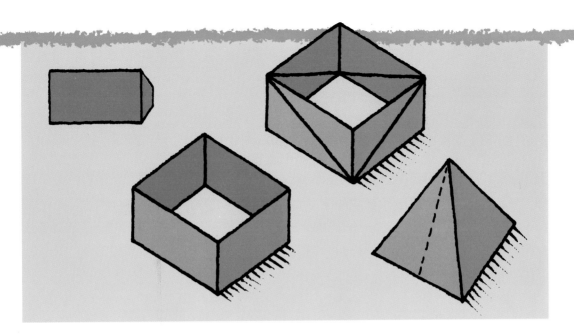

There are lots of other interesting ways to build tetrahedra. One way is to start with four 17cm x 10cm rectangles cut from card, with a tab on one edge of each. The tabs are glued and joined to make a hollow box.

The diagonals are drawn as shown in the diagram, and good creases are made along the diagonals. Then the shape is folded to make a tetrahedron.

CHALLENGE:

Can you make a tetrahedron from an old envelope?

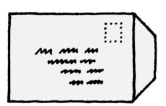  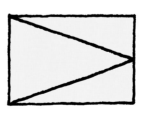 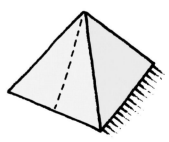

It is best to use a large brown envelope.
- Start by cutting across the envelope at the open end.
- Mark the mid-point of the open edge.
- Draw lines from here to the two opposite corners.
- Score and fold these lines firmly.
- Now hold up the envelope firmly, and blow into it.

SPHERE AND HEMISPHERE

A **sphere** is a perfectly rounded
three-dimensional shape. It always
looks the same from whichever direction
you look at it. If an object is shaped like a
sphere, it is described as **spherical.**
It is different from most other
three-dimensional shapes
because it has just one
curved face, and no
vertices or edges.

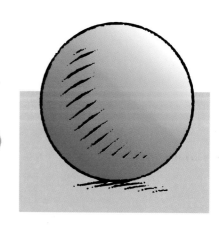

A ball is a sphere.
As a snooker ball is
perfectly rounded,
it can roll in a neat
straight line.

Many games and sports
use spherical shapes.

The width of a sphere is called its diameter. To measure the diameter of a sphere, you can place two blocks firmly either side of the sphere, then use a ruler to measure the distance between the two blocks. This will be the diameter of the sphere. The radius of the sphere, which is the distance from the centre of the sphere to its surface, is half the diameter.

A **hemisphere** has a curved face and a flat circular face.

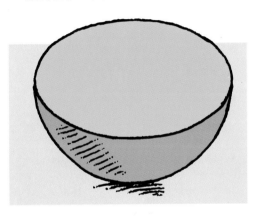

Many fruits are almost spherical. When a sphere is sliced in half, each half is called a hemisphere.

TO DO:

Design and make an open box to hold four table-tennis balls. Design one for six table-tennis balls.

GLOSSARY

arc	Part of the boundary of a circle.
circumference	The distance around the boundary of a circle.
chord	A straight line which divides a circle into two pieces.
cone	A 3D shape with a pointed top and a circular base.
cylinder	A prism with a circular face at each end.
cube	A cuboid whose faces are all squares.
cuboid	A 6-faced polyhedron whose faces are rectangles. A 'box' shape.
decagon	A 10-sided polygon.
decahedron	A 10-faced polyhedron.
diameter	The length of a chord of a circle which passes through the centre.
dodecahedron	A 12-faced polyhedron.
equilateral triangle	A triangle whose sides are all the same length.
hemisphere	Half a sphere.
heptagon	A 7-sided polygon.
hexagon	A 6-sided polyhedron.
irregular polygon	A polygon which is not regular.
isosceles triangle	A triangle which has two equal sides.
kite	A quadrilateral with two pairs of adjacent equal sides.
nonagon	A 9-sided polygon.
octagon	An 8-sided polygon.
octahedron	An 8-faced polyhedron.
parallel lines	Lines which though extended in both directions will never meet.

parallelogram	A quadrilateral with two pairs of opposite parallel sides.
pentagon	A 5-sided polygon.
pentahedron	A 5-faced polyhedron.
plane shape	Another name for a flat (2D) shape.
polygon	A 2D shape with straight sides.
polyhedron	A 3D shape with faces which are polygons.
prism	A 3D shape with an identical polygon face at each end, joined by rectangle faces.
pyramid	A 3D shape with a pointed top and a flat base.
quadrilateral	A 4-sided polygon.
radius	The distance from the centre of a circle to its boundary.
rectangle	A parallelogram with four right angles.
regular polygon	A polygon for which all sides are the same length and all angles are the same size.
right-angled triangle	A triangle with has a right angle.
rhombus	A parallelogram with four equal sides.
scalene triangle	A triangle whose sides are all of different lengths.
segment	A piece of a circle cut off by a chord.
sphere	A perfectly rounded 3D shape. A 'ball' shape.
square	A rectangle with four equal sides.
tetrahedron	A polyhedron with four triangular faces.
trapezium	A quadrilateral with one pair of parallel sides.
triangle	A 3-sided polygon.
vertex	The corner of a shape (2D or 3D).

INDEX

ANSWERS

p4 Rectangle, oval, pentagon, parallelogram.
Quadrilateral: 4 sides, 4 vertices; pentagon: 5 sides,
5 vertices; hexagon: 6 sides, 6 vertices

p5 Shape 1: 8 vertices, 6 faces, 12 edges
Shape 3: 6 vertices, 5 faces, 9 edges

p6 Hexagon, pentagon, quadrilateral, triangle

p7 Square

p9 **Challenge:**

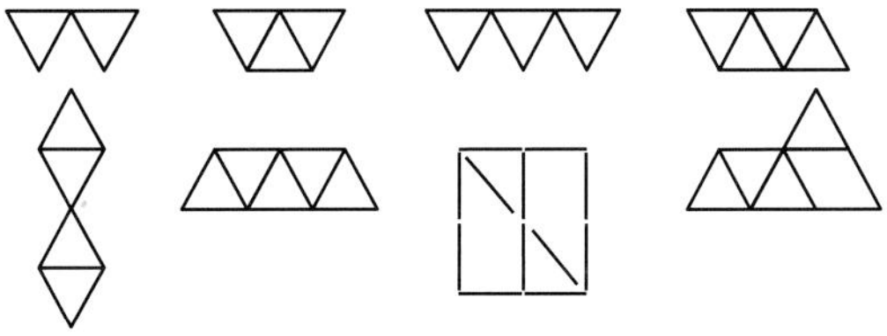

p11 Triangles - top row: right-angled and isosceles,
isosceles, right-angled, right-angled and isosceles.
bottom row: isosceles, scalene, scalene,
right-angled and isosceles

p12 **Challenge:**
The tennis court has 9 rectangles.

p13 2 by 5, 5 by 3, 5 by 6, 3 by 6, 1 by 4

To do:

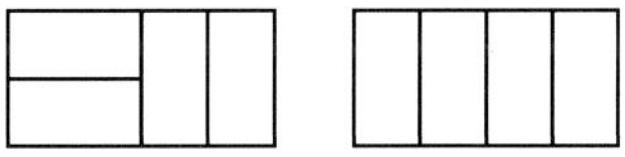

A few suggestions are:

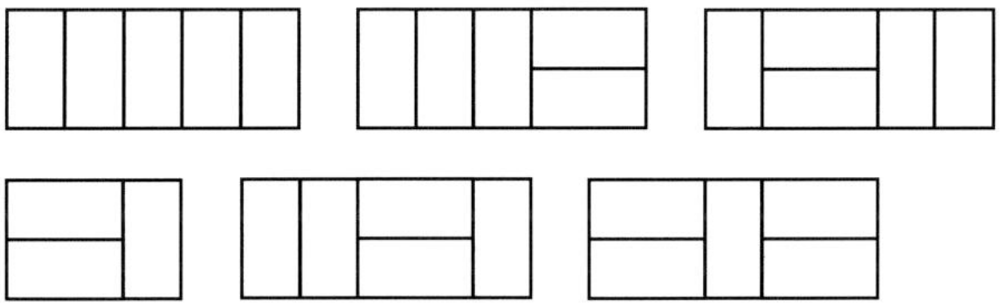

p15 64 small squares

p17

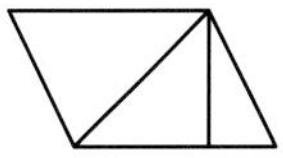

p18 The shape at top centre is not a trapezium

p19

47

p21   **Challenge:**
top row - trapezium, parallelogram, rectangle, kite
2nd row - quadrilateral, trapezium, quadrilateral, square
3rd row - square, square, kite, trapezium
bottom row - parallelogram, quadrilateral, kite, quadrilateral

p25   10 chords and 5 arcs.

p26   The faces are square, triangle,and pentagon.

p27   **Challenge:**
2 regular polyhedra - cube and tetrahedron.

To do:
Cuboid, tetrahedron, octahedron

p28

p29   1000 cubic centimetres

p30

p31

p33   12 cubes, 15 cubes, 24 cubes

Challenge:
With 24 bricks you can build, 2 by 3 by 4; 1 by 3 by 8;
1 by 1 by 24; 1 by 4 by 6.
With 36 bricks you can build seven cuboids: 1 by 1 by 36;
2 by 2 by 9; 1 by 2 by 18; 1 by 4 by 9; 1 by 3 by 12;
2 by 3 by 6; 1 by 6 by 6.

p34   The pyramids, from left to right are: triangular based - 4;
pentagonal based - 6 faces; hexagonal based - 7 faces;
square based - 5 faces.

p37   Hexagonal prism, triangular, prism, hexagonal prism

Challenge:
The net on the left does not make a prism.

p38   The cylindrical tins are the two tomato soup and the apple
juice tins.